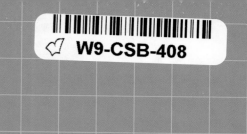

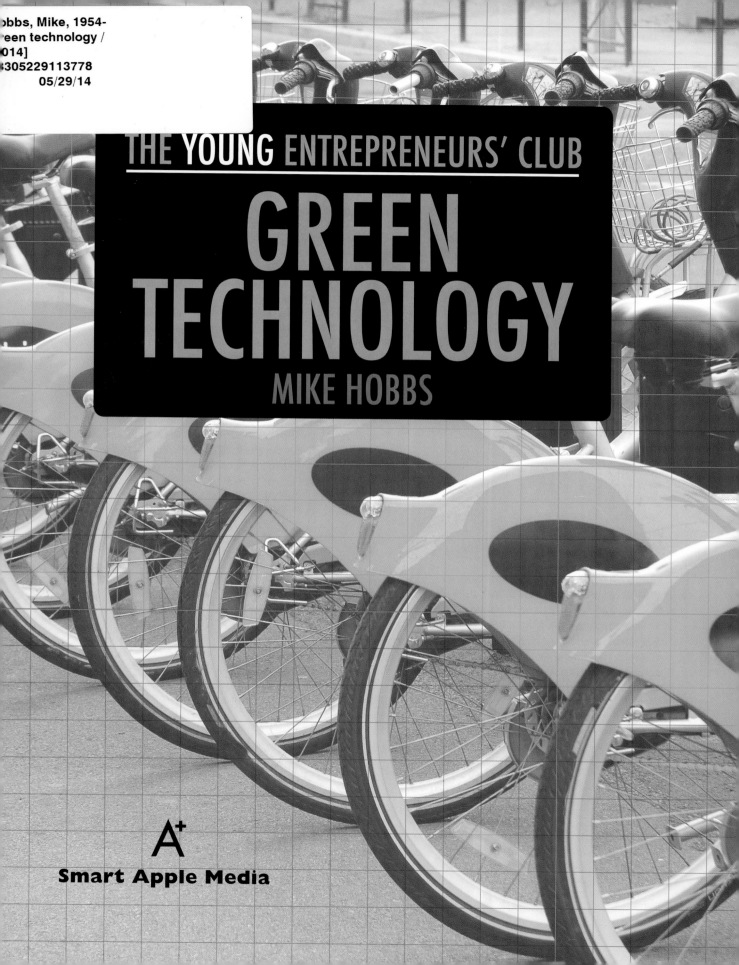

THE YOUNG ENTREPRENEURS' CLUB

GREEN TECHNOLOGY

MIKE HOBBS

A+
Smart Apple Media

Published by Smart Apple Media,
an imprint of Black Rabbit Books
P.O. Box 3263, Mankato, Minnesota 56002
www.blackrabbitbooks.com

Published by arrangement with the
Watts Publishing Group LTD, London.

Library of Congress Cataloging-in-Publication Data

 Green technology / Mike Hobbs.
pages cm. -- (The young entrepreneurs' club)
Summary: "Students interested in eco-
technology learn what it takes to become
young entrepreneurs in the industry. Successful
inventors of environmental and "green" gadgets
and products are spotlighted, and instructions
are given to jumpstart ideas and business plans.
Questions throughout the book challenge critical
thinking"-- Provided by publisher.
Audience: Grade 7 to 8.
Includes index.
ISBN 978-1-59920-925-8 (library binding) --
ISBN 978-1-62588-965-2 (ebook)
1. Green products--Juvenile literature.
2. Green technology--Juvenile literature.
3. Entrepreneurship.--Juvenile literature.
4. Green movement--Economic aspects--Juvenile
literature. 5. New business enterprises--Juvenile
literature. I. Title.
HD9999.G772H63 2013
 660.028'6--dc23
                              2013000082
Series Editor: Paul Rockett
Editor: Hayley Fairhead
Consultant: David Gray
Design: Simon Borrough
Picture Research: Diana Morris

Printed in the United States at
Corporate Graphics in North Mankato, Minnesota
PO1589/2-2013

9 8 7 6 5 4 3 2 1

Picture credits: Chris Anderson/Shutterstock: 28b;
Angaza Design www.angazadesign.com : 33; Adrian
Arbib/Alamy: 19c; Ariwasabi/Shutterstock: 7; BBOXX
Ltd www.bboxx.co.uk : 21; Mauro Beschi/Shutterstock:
22c; Bestweb /Shutterstock: 8; Holger Burmeister/
Alamy: 32c; Pavel Chelko/Shutterstock: 31bg; Robert
Churchill/istockphoto: 26; Climate Cars via Woodthorpe
Comms Ltd: 23; S. Dashkevych/Shuttertock: 24; Ecologic
www.ecologicfoodservice.com: 13; Ecoscraps http://
ecoscraps.net: 15t, 15b; Ecover www.ecover.com: 32b;
Equitable Origin www.equitableorigin.com: 27 inset,
27t; Feelgoodz www.feelgoodz.com: 29; Paul Glendell /
Alamy: 36bc; Leon Goedhart/istockphoto: 12; David
Gomez/istockphoto: 33; Levente Gyori/Shutterstock: 20t;
Hanna Kalenik/Shutterstock: 16bg; Justin Kasez12z/
Alamy: 30b; Michelle Kaufmann www.michellekaufmann.
com: 39t, 39b; Lsqrd42/Shutterstock: 38; mangostock/
Shutterstock: 20c, 20b; Dimitar Marmov/istockphoto:
17; MaxFX/Shutterstock: 10; MC Films/Rex Features:
34tr; Courtesy of Clay McInnis www.southernecogroup.
com: 25; Lissandra Melo/Shutterstock: 31cr; Nyul/
Dreamstime: 28t; olly/Shutterstock : 14; M. Panchecnko/
Shutterstock: 5, 22t; People Tree www.peopletree.co.uk :
34cl; Chayapol Plairaham/Shutterstock: 18; Isabel Poulin/
Dreamstime: 36bl; Project Better Place www.betterplace.
com: 35; Regreen Corporation www.regreencorp.com: 11;
Shopping Mall/Alamy: 30c; Stocknadia/Shutterstock: front
cover bg The Green Creation www.thegreencreation.com
: 37; Tupungato/Shutterstock: 16c; Twing /istockphoto:
22b; Vector Forever/Shutterstock: front cover c; Chris Watt
Photography: 9t; Angela Waye/Shuttertock: 32.

CONTENTS

What Is Green Technology?

The Green Technology Market

Green technology helps to provide goods or services that are **environmentally friendly**. The use of **fossil fuels** has caused damage to the planet in the form of **climate change**. The growing world population means that the planet's resources, like land and water, are needed by more and more people while the world is producing greater amounts of waste. Green **entrepreneurs,** called **ecopreneurs,** are trying to make goods or services that don't damage the environment. Not only that—the making, packaging, and distribution of green goods must also be done without harming the environment. Some of the main types of green technology are:

- Alternative fuels (not fossil fuels) and the vehicles that use them, such as **biofuels** or electric cars
- Renewable energy sources, such as energy from the sun, water, or wind
- Environmental goods and services, such as clothing made from natural **products**
- Waste conversion services, where solid waste is turned into a **biodegradable** material
- Building technologies, such as homes built from energy-efficient materials
- Low-carbon goods and technologies, such as foods that have been made and transported without releasing too much harmful carbon gas into the environment

There is a great deal of competition in this new market, but the opportunity is always there to break in with exciting new ideas. People are becoming much more aware of green issues.

Fact:

A recent study showed that the global market for green goods and services in 2007–08 was over $5 trillion. This world market is predicted to grow to approximately $7.2 trillion by 2014–15.

A survey of nine leading national markets in 2009 found that 89 percent of people would be more likely to buy green goods and services and 35 percent would pay a bit more to do so. In the United States, only 31 percent were ready to pay a bit extra for green goods.

CHALLENGE

In which areas of the green market do you think your ideas could make a difference?

Young Entrepreneurs
Recyclists

Roarke Hughes (left) and Niall Watson (right) of Scotland had a simple green idea. They were both 14 years old when they needed to earn £150 ($240) for their school trip. They did some research and found out that, because their council only collects paper, many people were throwing away stuff that could be recycled. They decided they would get on their bikes and cycle around their town, collecting trash for **recycling**. They charged £1 ($1.60) for each bag they collected.

They saved enough for the school trip but decided to keep their business going. Both of them are fully committed to helping the environment and figured out a way of increasing their income by combining their bicycle collection service with delivery of free range eggs from their own chickens. They had invested in the chickens after winning £2,000 ($3,200) from a children's award for green projects. The two were also the youngest finalists at the People and Environment Awards 2011, known as the "Green Oscars."

YOUR THOUGHTS

Why do you think their recycling plan was successful?

What Makes a Successful Ecopreneur?

What Is an Ecopreneur?

An entrepreneur is a person who takes a financial risk to bring a new idea to market. An ecopreneur brings a new green idea to market. It might help if the idea is yours but, wherever it comes from, you have to be the one who's going to try to find people to buy it. An ecopreneur invests time, money, and energy in developing an **eco-friendly** idea with the aim of making a **profit**. The product or service must be of benefit to the environment and be produced and distributed without harm to the planet.

The Skills You Need

There are many qualities you need to be successful. Perhaps the most important of these is a commitment to making a greener world and a knowledge of environmental issues. You have to be clever, inventive, and determined. In order to convince investors and the buying public that your green business idea will succeed, you must show great attention to detail. If you can match all this with the ability to work hard, and a knowledge of what the public will like, then you'll be an ecopreneur.

CHALLENGE

Think of some ideas for your own green business, such as making natural products or providing environmentally friendly transportation.

Young Entrepreneurs
ReGreen Corporation

Sean Neman (left) and David Duel (middle) of Los Angeles were both 22 and studying business together at the University of Southern California when they had their green business idea. Many companies and organizations were eager to go green but didn't know how to do it. They convinced their friend Kevin Refoua (right), age 23, who shared their passion for environmental issues to join them. Their start-up, the ReGreen Corporation, helps the environment by advising companies on the best ways of saving energy while also saving those companies money.

They started ReGreen in 2008, helped by $400,000 they raised from family and friends. They have become successful through determination and hard work. The trio have quickly built the company to the point where it has over 100 employees, 3,000 customers, and a turnover of $15 million in 2011.

YOUR THOUGHTS

What qualities did the ecopreneurs behind ReGreen Corporation show that made them successful?

Green Brainstorming

Coming Up with Ideas

So, as an ecopreneur, you feel that the world is going to have to get greener and you want to do your part to help. What ideas do you have? Do you have a great new way of producing energy from natural sources or a car powered by kitchen waste? Ask your friends and family what they think of your ideas. Test them out and forget those that don't work. Now get working on the best idea and try to make it perfect. There can be quite a lot of differences between your first idea and what you finally come up with.

CHALLENGE

List four ideas for a green business in the area of energy-saving goods and explain how you would test them.

Find Out if It Works

What you need to do next is to sort out the details of your service or develop a working model of your product. Once you've planned it, you need to test the model or do a trial run of your service to see whether it actually does what you want it to do. Remember, you're not worried so much about how your product looks at the moment. You're focusing on how it works, and whether it's likely to stand up to being used again and again. Make sure your testing doesn't harm the environment.

Young Entrepreneur
EcoLogic Products

Lawrence Ohlman III of Toledo, Ohio, uses natural plant fibers to make cutlery instead of metal or plastic. It all started when Lawrence was researching the use of plants and food waste to make flower pots. He realized what a good idea it would be if people could have a totally environmentally friendly way of eating. He checked around, and no one else seemed to be doing this at the time. So he set up EcoLogic Products in 2007 and tested how natural plant fibers could be used in packaging for hot and cold food.

EcoLogic Products became the first company whose tableware, made from natural plant fibers, was approved by the US Food and Drug Administration. What's more, the tableware is biodegradable, which means that it breaks down over a period of time, and then can be returned to the earth without any landfill problems. The company is now moving into **sustainable** food packaging.

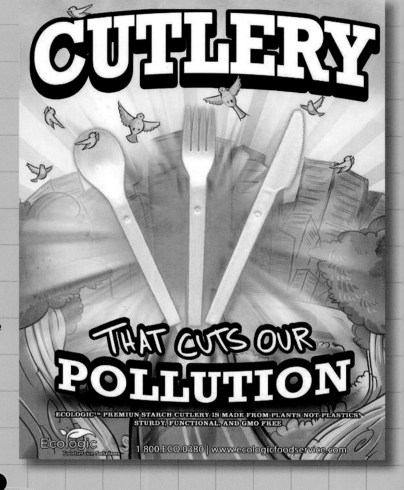

CUTLERY

THAT CUTS OUR POLLUTION

ECOLOGIC™ PREMIUN STARCH CUTLERY IS MADE FROM PLANTS NOT PLASTICS. STURDY, FUNCTIONAL, AND GMO FREE

Ecologic Foodservice Solutions

1.800.ECO.0380 | www.ecologicfoodservice.com

all natural, plant based, renewable and responsible picnicware

Ecologic

Premium Biobased Utensils
24ct
SPOON

MADE FROM PLANTS NOT PLASTIC

YOUR THOUGHTS

Other than the food temperature, what else did Lawrence need to consider when he was testing his cutlery?

Researching Your Market

CHALLENGE

You might have had a business idea for protecting gardens from pests with natural products. What five questions would you ask members of the public to find out if it might work?

Primary and Secondary Research

Now you need to find out whether there will be enough people likely to buy your new green product or use the service. This is where **market research** comes in. Before you spend money bringing your idea to life, check around to see whether people are interested in it. How important are green issues to your **potential market**? How much more are people willing to spend on a green product as opposed to a cheaper product that may harm the environment?

You have got to do some classic market research to find your answers, and there are two main types. Primary research involves finding new information by actually walking around and checking things or even standing in the street and asking questions. This will only be relevant to you if you want to sell your green goods to the public and would like some feedback from them. Secondary research involves finding and using existing information in the library or on the Internet.

Young Entrepreneurs
EcoScraps

When they went to one of their local restaurants in 2009, Brandon Sargent, Daniel Blake (left), and Craig Martineau (right) from Provo, Utah, found that massive amounts of food were being thrown away—literally. They checked and found that all the other diners and restaurants were doing the same thing, and that there would be no competition to get ahold of the leftovers.

Now all they needed to do was to find out what they could do with the scraps, and after some trials, they managed to develop a way of turning them into **organic** compost. With these leftovers to work with, they researched who was looking for environmentally friendly compost in Utah and found there was a potential market. As a result, they were able to develop their business, EcoScraps, which recycles food waste from stores and restaurants throughout Utah to be used as **fertilizer**. Now they have 18 employees, have won various awards, and they have also expanded into Arizona and Colorado, and are looking to grow further.

YOUR THOUGHTS

Which type of research, primary or secondary (or both), do you think the EcoScraps founders carried out? What did they learn?

Finding Start-up Funds

Who Can Help You?

However great your idea, you'll need some money to help get you started. Explore all the different places and people you can approach for **start-up funds**. Don't forget the obvious ones, such as friends and family, along with banks, government loan programs, and business investors. Then begin working out a proper **budget**, including all the **costs** you'll have to pay. Be realistic about your **sales**, because anyone who invests in your business will want to know the likely figures.

◀ **Banks and other investors will need to see a clear financial plan that they believe you can achieve.**

CHALLENGE

List 10 people you can approach to try to get funds, and rank them in order of the amount they may invest and how difficult it may be for you to approach them.

You may be able to get a loan or a grant to start a new business. This is especially true for young entrepreneurs. Go to the local library or look up new business incentives on the Internet. There may be various prizes for new green ideas or businesses available. As environmental issues become increasingly important, governments, businesses, and individuals are all keen to **promote** green business ideas through awards and prizes.

Young Entrepreneurs
Alphabet Energy

Matthew Scullin and Peidong Yang of Berkeley, California, were able to get funding for their company, Alphabet Energy, through grants and investors. Their **thermoelectric** technology turns heat **emissions** like those from power stations into electricity. This cuts heat waste, helps produce power at low cost, and is easy to install. Investors were interested in Alphabet Energy not only because it was a great idea, but also because it needed only a small amount of funding with the potential to grow into a billion dollar business. The pair also set clear goals, which they have gone on to achieve.

When they started the company in 2009, Matthew and Peidong received $320,000 in Small Business Innovation Research grants, raised the same in angel funding (from investors who help start-ups), and won awards from the Clean Tech Open (including the People's Choice and California Sustainability awards). As a result, Alphabet Energy was able to get funding of $1 million from Claremont Creek Ventures and the CalCEF Clean Energy Angel Fund. It has recently received a massive $12 million from a group led by TPG Biotech, followed by a further growth fund of $2 million from Hercules Technology Growth Capital.

YOUR THOUGHTS

Do you think the Alphabet Energy founders will have any problems because they have raised money from so many people? What might those problems be?

Developing Your Product

Getting Ready for the Market

You've tested your green idea, researched your market, and found some money to get you going. Now you have to take account of the research. You need to design your product (or get someone else to do it for you) so it looks as exciting as possible without taking away any of its ability to work. For instance, you may want to develop your idea for an eco-friendly protector from garden pests, but you have to make sure it is harmless to plant life. Its design should be simple, user-friendly, and attractive.

Now's the time to work hard at improving your product or service—you must have it as close to perfect as you can when you decide to **launch**. This can cause delays, which is hard when you know how fast things change in the business world. However, it's very important that you take time to test your product carefully and that you continue to act in an environmentally responsible way. Get advice from green-product designers if you can.

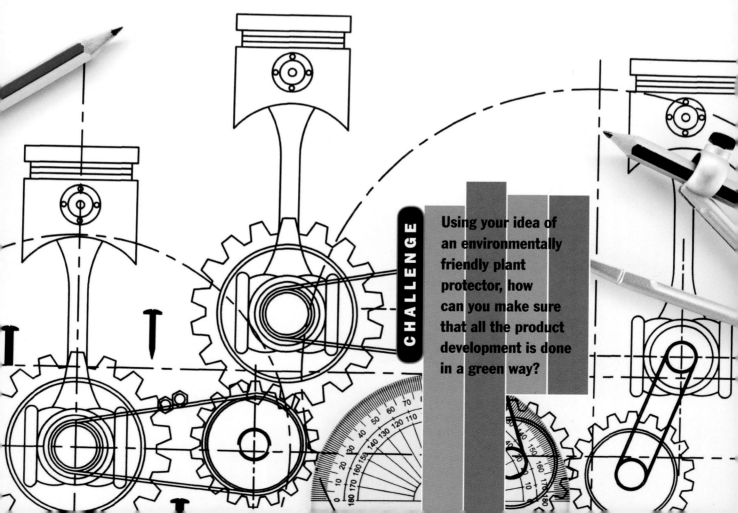

CHALLENGE

Using your idea of an environmentally friendly plant protector, how can you make sure that all the product development is done in a green way?

Inspiring Entrepreneur
Freeplay

Trevor Baylis (below) of the United Kingdom, got the idea for developing a clockwork wind-up radio from a TV show in 1989 about AIDS. The show said that the disease in Africa could best be fought by giving out information via radio. Trevor invented a clockwork radio in his workshop, knowing that electricity and batteries were hard to get in many parts of Africa. He then worked on developing the **prototype** but it was rejected many times until, five years later, it finally appeared on a BBC TV show called *Tomorrow's World* and got noticed. After that, he developed his original Baygen radios into the cheaper, smaller Freeplay model used throughout Africa and beyond. He has received many awards for his work.

These days Trevor has decided to help out young entrepreneurs and inventors. The company Trevor Baylis Brands helps entrepreneurs, particularly those involved with green technology, to get protection for their ideas (often through **patents**) and to find a market for their products.

YOUR THOUGHTS

Do you think it was helpful to Trevor that it took so long for his idea to be accepted? Why?

Making the Most of Being Green

Using the Environment as a Selling Point

One of the benefits of green technology is that it is being developed to meet a real need—the protection of the planet. So there are good environmental reasons why your product is important and you must learn to focus on these and use them as part of your business plan. Maybe you've had an idea for a way of cleaning cars without wasting water. What are the benefits? Your passion for the business to succeed has to be backed up by environmental arguments.

▲ **Maybe your idea will help to conserve the world's resources.**

CHALLENGE

You're trying to develop a waste recycling service. Write down three reasons why your idea will be useful to the planet.

You've already carried out your primary and secondary market research, but now you need to get down to some scientific research. You don't have to make things too complicated. In fact, it's much better if you don't. What you're looking for are a few clear reasons why what you're providing will contribute towards a greener environment. You'll need to present your ideas in a way that makes it easy for your potential customers (and investors) to understand.

Young Entrepreneurs

BBOXX Ltd

Christopher Baker-Brian, Laurent Van Houcke, and Mansoor Mohammad Hamayan (below), based in the United Kingdom, have been able to use their scientific knowledge to bring **solar energy** to the **developing world**. They launched their business, BBOXX Ltd, in 2009 when they were in their 20s.

The trio, who all studied at Imperial College (which specializes in technology and engineering), showed that a small battery box that stored solar energy would be a huge benefit to people who lived in countries where there was little or no electricity. Each box converts the sun's power into electricity for a home's lights (see inset below), TVs, phones, radios, etc. Originally part of e.quinox, a charity at Imperial College, the company is now separate from the charity and is free to make a profit. Their products have now launched in Iraq, Pakistan, Rwanda, and the Democratic Republic of Congo. The members of the company won the Shell Livewire Young Entrepreneurs of the Year award for 2010.

YOUR THOUGHTS

Do you think it was easier for the BBOXX founders to develop their business plan because they were all at a science-focused university? Why?

Know Your Competition

Rivals in Your Market

Green technology is relatively new, but already very popular. You may not have direct competition, but lots of businesses are after the same market. So there will probably be others doing roughly similar things, and you must check them out. Learn about them, find out what problems they've faced, and try to learn from their mistakes. It really is true that the more you research, the better the chance you have to succeed.

▲ **A city bike rental program would need to consider competition from taxis, buses, and other bike rental companies.**

CHALLENGE

You're planning to move into the natural soap products market. Who do you think are going to be your three main competitors? List their strengths and weaknesses.

You probably noticed some potential **competitors** when you did your primary research. Now is the time to look at them closely, if you haven't done so already. What advantages do you have over them? What disadvantages do you have? Discover as much as you can about any **rivals** who might affect your success.

Young Entrepreneur
Climatecars

Nicko Williamson (left) of London set up Climatecars, his special green taxi service in 2007, when he was just 22 years old. Nicko uses Toyota Prius cars, which can run on electricity when traveling up to 30 mph (48 km/h). It is hardly ever possible to go faster in London, so the cars almost always run on electricity. These cars pump out 60 percent less carbon dioxide than diesel-powered taxi cabs.

When Nicko launched Climatecars, a rival green taxi service was already in operation. Nicko realized that if he aimed his business at corporate clients, he could get an edge over his rivals. Nicko's cars look professional and he offers his customers a competitive fixed-rate fee. His drivers open doors for passengers and offer them bottled water for the journey. Corporate clients have been drawn to Climatecars's professional, competitively priced service. The company now has over 100 vehicles. Nicko was named Ernst & Young 2011 Young Entrepreneur of the Year and BusinessGreen's Young Sustainability Executive of the Year 2011.

YOUR THOUGHTS

Green taxi services are becoming even more popular. In what other ways could Nicko get ahead of his rivals?

Financial Planning

Future Costs, Sales, and Profits

You'll find you now need to make further financial plans to show where your profits are coming from. Remember, your profit is the money you bring in minus your costs. You may also need to bring in more financial investors. You'll have to ensure good **cash flow**, keeping a regular supply of money coming in. There will be more chance of getting long-term investments if you've got a proper financial plan, showing what these backers will get in return and when they'll get it.

Included in a financial plan will be:

- Amount you need to invest in equipment
- Amount you'll have to pay on weekly running costs
- Other estimated costs
- Predicted sales for your first year

Also include when you hope to be able to start paying back your investors.

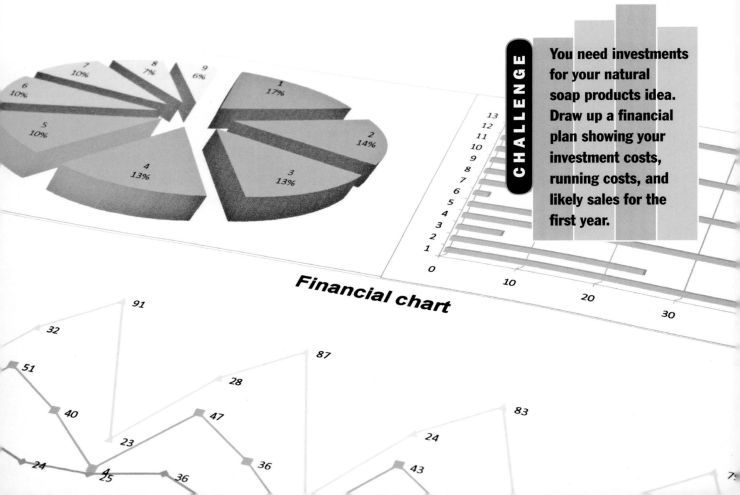

Financial chart

CHALLENGE

You need investments for your natural soap products idea. Draw up a financial plan showing your investment costs, running costs, and likely sales for the first year.

Young Entrepreneur
Southern Eco

Originally, Clay McInnis of Montgomery, Alabama, set out to find a way of using biodiesel in his family's construction business. His biodiesel fuel is made from plant oil and used vegetable oil collected free from local restaurants. The cost of making it is less than one-third of the cost of diesel oil. It produces less harmful gases and causes less wear on engines. After getting started in his early 20s, he was able to build on home support and publicity from a *Businessweek* award to find backers interested in the small investment needed for equipment and the low running costs. He was then able to sell his small biodiesel equipment and his fuel to local schools, colleges, businesses, and corporations.

As well as making the fuel himself, he made all the equipment until the business grew too much for him alone. One of the partners for his company, Southern Eco, is the California-based Springboard Biodiesel, which makes the equipment that he now sells. Clay was a finalist in Bloomberg *Businessweek's* 2011 Young Entrepreneur of the Year competition and is committed to teaming up with local organizations.

YOUR THOUGHTS

Why do you think investors were interested in Southern Eco?

Building Your Team

CHALLENGE

Your idea for soap from natural products is taking off. Which three areas of the business do you need the most help with?

Choosing People to Help Your Vision Come True

In business, you have to work with people. No one can do everything. So it's important that you build a strong team to work with you, and that you make sure everyone knows what their tasks are. You'll need people with technical knowledge, people who know about the environment, and people with selling skills—and that's just for starters. You may have to interview people to fill other jobs in your team. List what their responsibilities will be and what type of person you want.

Once you've chosen your team, make sure everyone knows what their roles are, and that they all communicate and listen to what others have to say. The second thing you must do is to learn to manage your time effectively. Everyone is going to want you to make a decision on all sorts of issues. You have to be able to decide when a problem needs to be dealt with urgently and what problems can wait.

Young Entrepreneurs
Equitable Origin

David Portiz (above) and Christian Seale of Providence, Rhode Island, put together the right team to grow their company Equitable Origin. The company looks at the environmental backgrounds of oil and gas providers to see how green they are. Equitable Origin started in 2009 while David was finishing at Brown University and Christian was waiting to go to Harvard Business School. Their idea was to set up a green standard that oil and gas companies had to meet.

David and Christian soon realized they needed to hire people with special skills. They wanted people who were committed to the same green values, but also with knowledge of the industry and the ability to rate the performance of companies fairly. They realized that they had to bring in experienced people to help out and they spent time and effort getting people with the right personalities as well as skills. They now have 11 employees and 4 consultants, with offices in Ecuador as well as Providence, New York, and Washington.

YOUR THOUGHTS

Why do you think that experienced people were needed in this business?

Learn to be Decisive

Making the Right Call

You'll probably have to be the leader of your green business and that means you'll have to make plenty of tough decisions. Listen to what people on your team have to say, but remember it's your business and your responsibility. This isn't something that anyone will expect you to learn overnight. It takes time and practice.

A few mistakes are forgivable in the early days as you hone problem-solving skills. When you're tackling a problem, it's up to you to see the big picture. Some problems are specific to the green market, such as making sure that while distributing your product, you are using low-carbon vehicles that don't have to travel long distances. You need to look at the impact on the environment of any decisions you make as well as how it may affect your customers.

CHALLENGE

Write down three main areas in which you think you'll have to take the lead and make decisions in your new business.

Young Entrepreneur
Feelgoodz

Kyle Berner of New Orleans picked up various lessons on leadership as he gradually managed to make his business selling shoes made from rubber, hemp, and bamboo successful. Feelgoodz shoes are flip-flops made from 100 percent natural Thai materials. Kyle pays the farmers fairly to grow sustainable rubber trees and he makes the shoes biodegradable.

He founded his company in 2007 when he was 27 and learned that promoting social and economic growth in Thailand would also make his flip-flops stand out in a crowded marketplace. Kyle has followed the example of how entrepreneur Blake Mycoskie makes a charitable contribution for every pair of TOMS shoes he sells. Kyle gives a small percentage of his profits to Phitsanulok (the place in Thailand where he used to live).

YOUR THOUGHTS

What leadership qualities are shown by Kyle Berner?

Make a Marketing Plan

Green Marketing Principles

You will need to have a very clear **marketing plan** if you want to be successful. Remember that running a green business gives you a strong base for promoting your product. Draw up a marketing plan that includes every part of the **marketing mix**. The aim of the plan is for you to spell out exactly how you are going to attract your target audience to buy your goods. Make sure the plan is closely linked to your budget and is environmentally friendly. Use recycled paper for promotional leaflets and posters, or use social media networks that don't use up the Earth's resources.

Once you've decided on your plan, you need to put it into action. To do this, it's often helpful to think of the four Ps:

Product—what your product offers and what sets it apart from its competition (e.g. clear use of the environmental benefits).

Price—what your customers will be prepared to pay for the product (e.g. will people pay more for green products?).

Place—how and where you are going to sell your product—in shops, supermarkets, online, or all three, bearing in mind what's best for the environment.

Promotion—how to reach your market most effectively. This can include **advertising**, PR, direct mail, and personal selling. Make sure you use the most eco-friendly way of promoting your product.

CHALLENGE You are about to launch green car cleaning service. Draft a marketing plan, using the principles of the four Ps.

◄ Make sure you use green posters, bags, and fixtures inside your shops.

Young Entrepreneur
Keep It Green Landscaping

In 2010, Adam Morris of Ottawa, Canada, was just 18 when his love of the environment and healthy living led him to begin his green business. Keep It Green Landscaping is a sustainable and conservation-focused business with a specific aim: to protect the small amounts of natural areas in our towns and cities today. Adam developed his marketing ideas, using this green angle in a market that was not crowded with competition, in order to ensure his landscaping business would succeed.

At first the business grew only by word-of-mouth, but Adam is now using social media networks to bring in clients who share his green values. He also uses charity events, community seminars, and targeted online coupons as other ways to find his likely customers. He has taken advice from many nonprofit and community organizations who are there to help young entrepreneurs.

YOUR THOUGHTS

Which of the four Ps do you think Adam has used most effectively?

Making Your Story Heard

Attracting Your Target Customers

Before you launch your green product, you need to make sure that as many likely customers as possible know about it. Obviously your green angle will be central to your story. Use a mixture of newspaper, radio, online, and TV advertising (if you've got the budget) with social media networking to get your message out. See that your advertising is in the right place and reaching the right people.

But that's not the only way. What you do to promote your invention may be just as important. If you've done your research, you'll know your target market. Now you must find the best ways to reach it. Plan your advertising campaign, and support it with some promotional work, such as offering free samples. Advertising aims to get your product in the right media, either in print or online, to grab your customers' attention. Publicity means using events or promotions to put your name in the public eye.

CHALLENGE

Your natural soap business needs to make its potential customers aware of its products. What is the best way to get your story heard?

Young Entrepreneurs
Angaza Design

Lesley Silverthorn (below) and Bryan Duggan from San Francisco, California, founded Angaza Design in 2010 when they were 24 to bring help to the poor in East and West Africa, Central America, India, and Afghanistan. The company designs systems to help the poor, such as solar-powered products for lighting households that are without electricity. Lesley, an ex-engineering consultant, wanted to do something that would help people in the developing world.

YOUR THOUGHTS

Has the Angaza team chosen the best way to get its story heard?

Angaza is run by a team of five, with Lesley now managing them. Angaza sells lighting systems that are designed to replace dangerous and expensive kerosene lamps. Angaza also makes cell phone chargers. Lesley plans to start selling to Kenya and Tanzania, as well as Nigeria in West Africa and Guatemala in Central America. To get her message across to her target markets, she spent a year traveling through these countries finding out about needs and raising awareness. She spoke to local government officials about her ideas and she met as many of her likely customers as possible.

Launch Time

Make the Most of Your Big Day

When it's time to launch your product, you need to make as big a song and dance as you can. You've got a great new green idea that is going to change the world and meet a real need, so you should be able to turn good publicity into sales.

▲ **Social media networks must be buzzing with the date you've set.**

If you've done some groundwork so that people are aware of your plans, then it will be easier to publicize the launch. Any advertising and publicity you do must be focused around the launch day. You want everyone to be talking about your product, including specialty green web sites. This is when you have a great chance to get people to try out your idea, maybe for a special price, without putting your long-term plans at risk. If there are any hitches, be sure to fix them as quickly as possible, because first impressions count.

Inspiring Entrepreneur
Project Better Place

Shai Agassi (above) of Tel Aviv, Israel, was able to convince major car manufacturer Renault-Nissan and the Israeli government to help him launch his green car so that the project got huge publicity. Shai had been a software entrepreneur and then a senior executive for many years. At a conference where everyone was encouraged to think up an idea that would be good for the earth, he first came up with his green car idea.

He realized that people would not be interested in electric cars until the batteries could be recharged as quickly as filling up with gas from a pump. He felt the solution was not to recharge but to replace the batteries, because that could be done so much more quickly. He was speaking about his plans for this when the President of Israel, Shimon Peres, was in the audience and encouraged him to set up Project Better Place. He gave government resources to Shai's project and that helped to bring in Renault-Nissan, whose managing director attended the launch with Ehud Olmert, Israel's Prime Minister.

YOUR THOUGHTS

How did the presence of Israel's Prime Minister and the head of Renault-Nissan help Shai's launch?

Boosting Sales and Distribution

What Can You Do Better?

Even though your business is up and running, you'll still have to work for every sale. You should always check your **sales figures** very carefully and see where you can improve. Are you using the right people to sell your products? Are you selling through the right **outlets** (shops and web sites)? How are online sales going? Are your potential customers buying? There may be reasons putting them off. Never be afraid to change things if they're not running smoothly. If you're using online sales, are you getting enough site visitors and converting them into buyers?

CHALLENGE

Your soap business is in its first year. How many sales did you expect? Are you achieving these and, if not, what can you do?

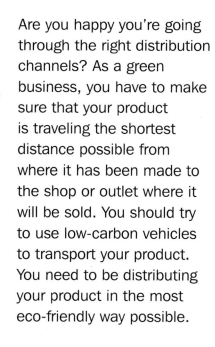

Are you happy you're going through the right distribution channels? As a green business, you have to make sure that your product is traveling the shortest distance possible from where it has been made to the shop or outlet where it will be sold. You should try to use low-carbon vehicles to transport your product. You need to be distributing your product in the most eco-friendly way possible.

Young Entrepreneur
The Green Creation

Smitha Prasad (right) from Fremont, California, started her business in 2010 when she was trying to find organic, sustainable baby clothes for her first child and felt that those on the market were badly designed and too expensive. She knew many other young parents felt the same and decided to fill this gap in the market. With a background in marketing and a skill for clothes design, she was able to come up with a line of attractive, sustainable cotton clothes and accessories for babies.

Smitha has made sure that her clothes are very competitively priced. She had contacts in India who helped her get the clothes manufactured in a **fairtrade** way in two Indian factories (see below). Smitha sells her clothes through The Green Creation web site, but she has also been able to distribute nationwide through many chains of baby stores. This means she can produce her goods in bulk. Because she sells through these stores and via the web site, she can attract sales from anyone who wishes to buy organic baby clothing.

YOUR THOUGHTS

Were there any other ways Smitha could have increased distribution and sales?

Turning Problems into Gains

Don't be Put Off by Setbacks

Nearly everyone has problems at the start of their business career, especially in new areas such as the green market. The important thing is to learn from your mistakes. Often you might be able to use what appears to be a problem to your advantage. Just make a few adjustments to your plan and try again—the key is never to give up! Keep trying different ways and means until you've got everything just how you want it.

This is the real world, and nobody expects perfection: an important person falls ill, there's a power outage affecting your online sales, a van breaks down, or there's a strike in your neighborhood. Some things are beyond your control. Just try to get around them as best you can. One of the important things to remember is you must always let your customers know if there are going to be any delays or changes to a plan. A simple message on your web site, or by phone, text, or email, will save you a lot of complaints and poor customer reviews.

CHALLENGE

You've launched your green car cleaning service. What's your biggest problem likely to be? How can you plan to turn it into a benefit?

Inspiring Entrepreneur
Michelle Kaufmann Studio

Michelle Kaufmann (below) of northern California, is an architect who had a vision. She wanted to make houses that were environmentally friendly. After working with famous architect Frank Gehry, she set up her own company, MK Designs, in 2002. She had seen that prices were too high for many people who wanted green homes. So she planned and delivered affordable green homes, making them available to everyone.

Michelle was given various awards and she was internationally recognized as an outstanding architect, but she was forced to close MK Designs in 2009 because of the **recession**. However, real entrepreneurs don't sit still for long, and in 2010 she opened her new architectural design business, Michelle Kaufmann Studio, a much smaller company that is working on smaller environmentally friendly projects.

YOUR THOUGHTS

How would you have reacted to the setback experienced by Michelle Kaufmann?

So What's Next?

Planning Your Follow-Up

Once your green idea has proven successful, you'll want to do it again—and you can! Start to think about how you can come up with your next green business move. You'll find it just as exciting, and you'll know more this time around.

Use your inventive mind to come up with new ideas or think of ways in which you can build on that success and expand your business. Don't be afraid to think big now that you know how it's done, within reason, of course. Remember, you can't do everything at once.

CHALLENGE

Your business selling natural soaps has been a success. List three potential green business areas you'd like to move into next.

Young Entrepreneurs
Solar City

Peter and Lyndon Rive of San Mateo, California, began their solar energy systems company, Solar City, in 2006 when they were in their 20s. Within a year, Solar City had become the leading provider of solar power in Californian homes. Soon after that, the company started to sell to businesses, government, and charities. By 2011, the company was the main provider of solar systems to homes in the United States.

However, they are not standing still. Solar City has agreed to a plan to provide solar energy for 120,000 military homes and has also entered the electric car charging market. The company is providing free charging for electric cars on the Los Angeles-San Francisco highway as publicity for their solar chargers, which they plan to sell to electric car owners.

YOUR THOUGHTS

Is electric car charging a sensible next step for a solar energy company? Why?

Glossary

advertising Images and text that interest people in your product or business.

biodegradable Something that can be broken down by bacteria or biological means.

biofuel Something of biological origin that is used as a fuel.

budget The amount of money you expect to spend and receive.

carbon dioxide Colorless, odorless gas, a mixture of oxygen and carbon, present in the air.

cash flow The money coming in and going out.

climate change The change in the Earth's weather patterns linked to the burning of fossil fuels.

competitor Someone who is competing with you to sell to consumers.

conserve Save or keep (often used for resources).

costs Everything you must spend to make sales.

developing world Generally refers to poor, non-industrial countries (e.g. in Africa and Asia).

eco-friendly (see environmentally friendly).

ecopreneur Someone who takes a financial risk on a green product or business in order to make a profit.

emissions Generally, the act of sending out (e.g. smoke as a by-product of energy).

entrepreneur Someone who takes a financial risk in order to make a profit.

environmentally friendly Not causing damage to the environment.

fairtrade The movement to help producers in the developing world gain a fair price for their goods.

fertilizer Something added to soil (or water) to help things grow more successfully.

fossil fuel Fuels such as coal and natural gas.

launch The moment you open your business or start selling your product.

manufacturer Someone who makes a product.

marketing mix The things you must do to market your goods.

marketing plan Describing your likely customers and how you'll sell to them.

market research Finding out if there's a market for your idea, or how it's doing.

organic Something that comes from living plants or animals, not from chemicals.

outlets Anywhere customers can buy your products.

patent The legal right to be the only producer of what you've invented.

potential market The people you might be able to sell to.

product Anything you make or produce for consumers to buy.

profit The amount of money you receive for sales, less the cost of making them.

promote Put your product or business in the minds of likely customers.

prototype The original version of your invention.

recession Hard financial times, when business is shrinking, not growing.

recycling Reusing products.

rival Someone who is competing with you to sell to consumers.

sales Everything you sell to consumers.

sales figures The total amount of sales reported regularly.

solar energy Energy stored from the sun's rays.

start-up funds Money to get your business going.

sustainable Maintained at a steady level without using up natural resources or causing damage.

thermoelectric The conversion of heat energy to electrical energy.

Further Information

Web Sites of Featured Entrepreneurs

Alphabet Energy **www.alphabetenergy.com**
Angaza Design **www.angazadesign.com**
BBOXX Ltd **www.bboxx.co.uk**
Climatecars **www.climatecars.com**
EcoLogic Foodservice Solutions
www.ecologicfoodservice.com
EcoScraps **http://ecoscraps.com**
Equitable Origin **www.equitableorigin.com**
Feelgoodz **www.feelgoodz.com**
Freeplay **www.freeplayenergy.com**
The Green Creation
www.thegreencreation.com

Keep It Green Landscaping
www.keepitgreenottawa.com
Michelle Kaufmann Studio
www.michellekaufmann.com
Project Better Place **www.betterplace.com**
Recyclists
http://therecycleboy.typepad.com
ReGreen Corporation
www.regreencorp.com
Solar City **www.solarcity.com**
Southern Eco
www.southernecogroup.com

Other Web Sites

www.bbc.co.uk/youngapprentice/
Official web site of *The Young Apprentice* series, where kids try out their skills to succeed in business.

www.green-technology.org/
Web site delivering up-to-date news on the development of green technologies.

www.youngentrepreneur.com/
Online forum for information and advice on being a young entrepreneur.

Books

Catch the Wind, Harness the Sun by Michael J. Caduto (Storey Pub., 2011)

Facts at Your Fingertips. Invention and technology: Power and Energy edited by Tom Jackson (Brown Bear Books, 2012)

Green-Collar Careers. Green Ways of Getting Around: Careers in Transportation by Diane Dakers (Crabtree Pub, 2012)

Note to parents and teachers: Every effort has been made by the publishers to ensure that these web sites are suitable for children, and that they contain no inappropriate or offensive material. However, because of the nature of the Internet, it is impossible to guarantee that the contents of these sites will not be altered.

Index